Better Homes and Gardens®

CHRISTMAS TRIMS

KIDS CAN MAKE

© Copyright 1988 by Meredith Corporation, Des Moines, Iowa.
All Rights Reserved. Printed in the United States of America.
First Edition. Second Printing, 1988.
Library of Congress Catalog Card Number: 87-63202
ISBN: 0-696-01640-0 (hardcover)
ISBN: 0-696-01641-9 (trade paperback)

BETTER HOMES AND GARDENS® BOOKS

Editor: Gerald M. Knox
Art Director: Ernest Shelton
Managing Editor: David A. Kirchner
Editorial Project Managers: James D. Blume,
    Marsha Jahns, Rosanne Weber Mattson

Senior Crafts Books Editor: Joan Cravens
Associate Crafts Books Editors: Liz Porter,
    Beverly Rivers, Sara Jane Treinen

Associate Art Directors: Neoma Thomas,
    Linda Ford Vermie, Randall Yontz
Assistant Art Directors: Lynda Haupert,
    Harijs Priekulis, Tom Wegner
Graphic Designers: Mary Schlueter Bendgen,
    Mike Burns, Brian Wignall
Art Production: Director, John Berg;
    Associate, Joe Heuer;
    Office Manager, Michaela Lester

President, Book Group: Jeramy Lanigan
Vice President, Retail Marketing: Jamie L. Martin
Vice President, Administrative Services: Rick Rundall

BETTER HOMES AND GARDENS® MAGAZINE
President, Magazine Group: James A. Autry
Vice President, Editorial Director: Doris Eby
Executive Director, Editorial Services: Duane L. Gregg

MEREDITH CORPORATION CORPORATE OFFICERS
Chairman of the Board: E.T. Meredith III
President: Robert A. Burnett
Executive Vice President: Jack D. Rehm

Christmas Trims Kids Can Make
Crafts Editor: Sara Jane Treinen,
    Elizabeth Porter
Editorial Project Manager: James D. Blume
Graphic Designers: Linda Ford Vermie,
    Harijs Priekulis
Electronic Text Processor: Paula Forest

Cover projects: See pages 18–19, 30–31, 44–45, 60–61.

CONTENTS

Parade Into Christmas

Let these high-stepping troopers march across a mantel of greenery and announce the holiday season at your house. Why not make one for your music teacher? It's a perfect gift and one you can make all by yourself.

Tin Soldiers and Brass Horns

Trace simple drawings onto tooling foil to create
a marching band or brass horns.

Materials you will need...

- ☐ Tooling foil with one side gold and the other silver
- ☐ Red string
- ☐ Felt-tip markers
- ☐ Old magazine
- ☐ Transparent tape
- ☐ Orange stick or cuticle stick
- ☐ Tracing paper
- ☐ Pencil
- ☐ Scissors

1 Select a horn or trumpet pattern from page 9. Use the pencil to trace the pattern onto tracing paper. Use a blue felt-tip marker to trace the pattern's blue lines. Use a red marker to color the pattern's red areas onto the tracing paper. Use a yellow marker to color the yellow areas. Tape the traced pattern onto the gold side of the foil. Place the foil on an old magazine. With a pencil, trace all of the lines to transfer them to the foil. Remove the pattern from the foil.

2 Turn the foil over so the silver side is up. Referring to your traced pattern, use a pencil to retrace just the *blue* lines onto the foil.

3 From the silver side, rub the orange stick firmly on the areas of the foil that are colored yellow on the pattern. This step gives the foil shape on the gold side.

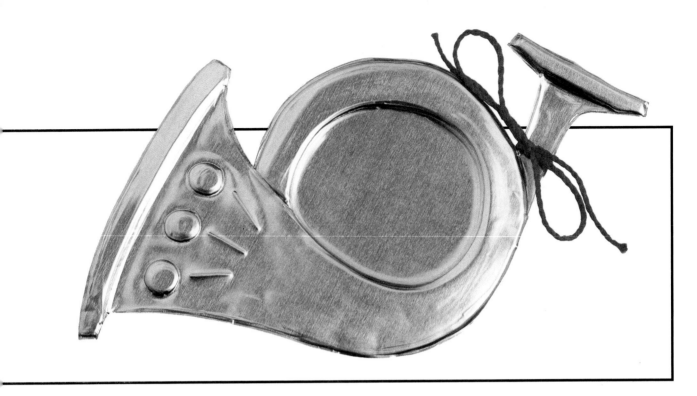

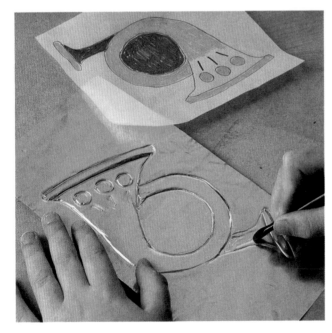

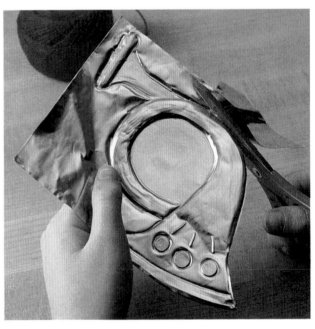

4 Turn the foil so the gold side is up. With the orange stick, push down all of the areas of the foil that are colored red on the pattern.

5 Cut out the design. Smooth any bends or rough edges with the orange stick.

6 Tie a 10-inch piece of red string in a bow around the neck of the horn.

Make the tin soldiers from the silver side of the tooling foil following steps 1–5. Then color the soldiers with the felt-tip markers.

Tin Soldiers and Brass Horns

Retrace the blue lines
on the back side

Rub the red areas
on the front side

Rub the yellow areas
on the back side

Make paper soldiers...

Trace the soldier patterns onto tan
oaktag, manila-folder paper (single
sheet), or other stiff paper. Color the
soldiers with crayons or felt-tip markers.
Cut out the shapes. Use them as
ornaments for your tree or to decorate a
package, as shown on pages 38–39.

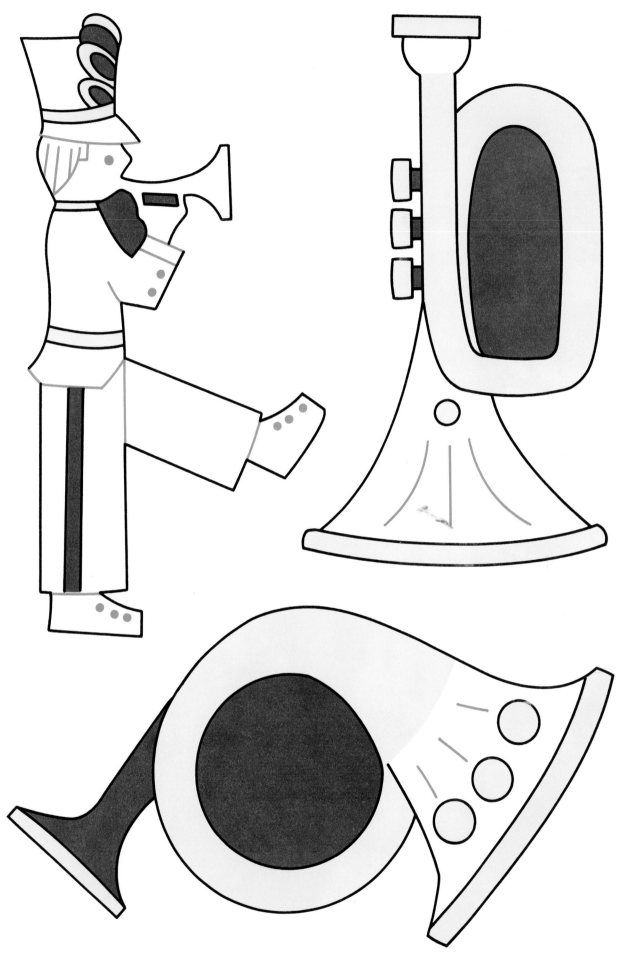

Make Your Own Cards

Lots of folks—teachers, grandmas and grandpas, even brothers and sisters—would love to receive a Christmas card that you made all by yourself. For a special touch, write your own holiday wishes on the inside of the card.

Marbleized Cards

Cut holiday shapes from bright-colored marbleized paper
to make your own cards and gift tags.

Materials you will need...

- [ ] Heavy, white watercolor paper
- [ ] Oil-based enamel hobby paints
- [ ] 9x13-inch pan
- [ ] Aluminum foil
- [ ] Drinking glass
- [ ] Paper towels
- [ ] Toothpicks
- [ ] Tweezers or tongs
- [ ] Tracing paper
- [ ] Scissors
- [ ] Paper punch
- [ ] Pencil

1 Line the pan with aluminum foil. Fill the pan with about 2 inches of water. Place the glass near the pan. Place paper towels under and all around the glass.

2 Stir the paint in the jar with a toothpick. Using the tip of the toothpick, tap drops of paint into the water. Swirl the paint in the water with the toothpick.

Try this...

Use two colors of paint to marbleize your paper. Simply tap two colors into the water. Swirl the paints with the toothpick. Then put your paper into the mixture and continue with Step 3.

Try this...

Use this same technique when dyeing Easter eggs. Just pour the water and paint into milk cartons or cottage cheese containers. Dunk blown-out eggs into the mixture. Place the eggs on paper towels to dry.

Make gift tags and holiday decorations...

Cut patterns from unfolded sheets of paper to make gift tags and tree ornaments. The star ornaments and holly and angel gift tags in the photo on pages 10 and 11 are made this way.

3 Lay the paper on top of the water. With the tweezers or tongs, lift the paper from the water. Shake off the excess water. Prop the paper against the glass to dry.

Tap more paint into the water to marbleize another piece of paper. To change colors, swirl paper towels on top of the water. They will remove the paint. Then tap another paint color onto the water.

4 Draw your own pattern or select a pattern of your choice from page 16. With the pencil, trace the pattern onto tracing paper. Cut out the tissue pattern. When the marbleized paper is dry, fold it in half. Lay the tissue pattern on top of the marbleized paper. Make sure the fold line of the pattern lies on top of the folded edge of the paper. Trace around the pattern. Cut out the design. Do not cut the folded edge. If you're making an angel, use the paper punch to trim the bottom of her skirt. Write your Christmas greeting inside the card.

13

Ribbon Cards

Scraps of paper satin ribbons decorate
these easy-to-make cards.

Materials you will need...

- ☐ ¼x9-inch pound-paper card stock
- ☐ Red, blue, yellow, and green *self-stick* paper satin ribbons
- ☐ ¾-inch gold star stickers
- ☐ Tracing paper
- ☐ Scissors
- ☐ Pencil

Try this...

- ●Use construction paper cut into 6¼x9-inch pieces instead of the pound paper.
- ●Use other paper satin ribbons and glue if you can't find the self-stick ribbons.

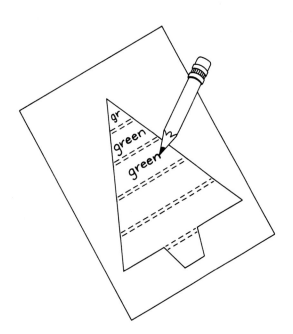

1 Select a pattern from page 17. Trace the pattern onto tracing paper. Trace both the solid and the broken lines. Write the color for each part of the pattern between the broken lines. Cut out the pattern along the *solid* line.

2 Fold the card paper in half. It should measure 4½x6¼ inches. Center the pattern on top of the folded card and use the pencil to lightly draw around the shape.

3 Cut the tissue pattern apart along the *broken* lines. The marked tissue pieces will be used as patterns to cut the ribbon.

4 Lay the patterns on the ribbons. Draw around each shape. Cut out the shapes.

14

You can make tree ornaments...

You can use these card designs for tree ornaments, too. Use an unfolded piece of construction paper that is slightly larger than the pattern you want to make. Follow the instructions for making the cards, below. Then when the ribbon pieces are in place, cut around the design about ¼ inch from the ribbon edges. Punch a hole in the top of the ornament. String an 8-inch piece of thread through the hole. Tie the thread ends in a knot to make a loop for hanging.

5 Working with one ribbon piece at a time, moisten the back of each piece and fasten it to the card within the drawn lines. When all pieces are in place, carefully erase the pencil markings that remain. Add the gold star sticker to the top of the tree.

Marbleized Cards

Angel

Use other patterns in the book...

Use the patterns on pages 68–71 for other card designs. And decorate your cards with bows or other trims. We used red pom-poms to decorate the tree card near the bottom of the photograph on page 11.

Reindeer

Candle

Place blue lines on fold of paper

Ribbon Cards

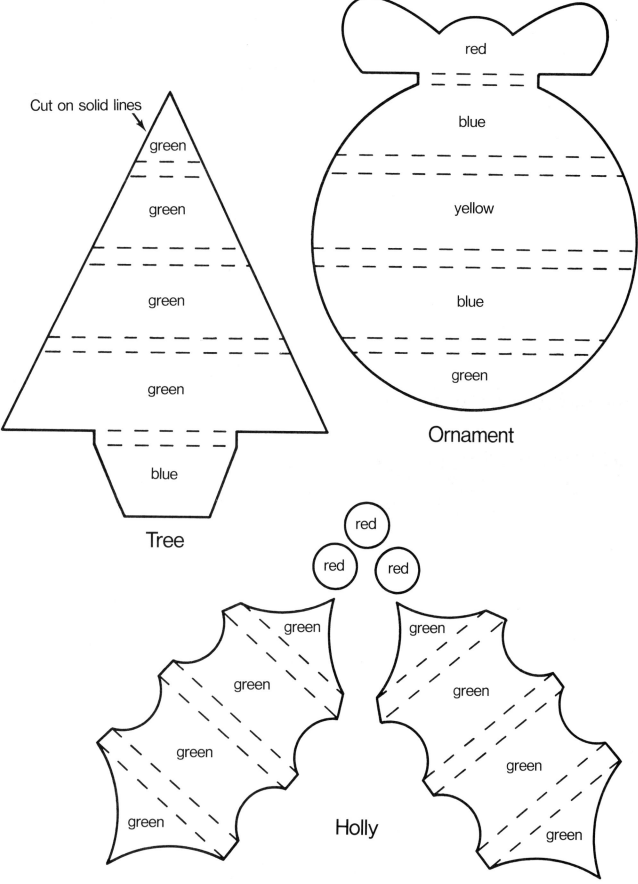

Cut on solid lines

green

green

green

green

blue

Tree

red

blue

yellow

blue

green

Ornament

red

red   red

green   green

green   green

green   green

green   green

green   green

Holly

17

Countdown To Christmas

You'll have fun waiting for Christmas if you make this Advent calendar before the season starts. Then, beginning on the first day of December, open a flap each day. When all the flaps are open, Christmas Day will have arrived.

Advent Calendar

Cut large and small evergreen trees from construction paper
to begin your three-dimensional Advent calendar.

Materials you will need to make the trees...

- ☐ 16 sheets of 9x12-inch green construction paper
- ☐ Rubber cement
- ☐ Pencil
- ☐ Tracing paper
- ☐ Scissors

- ☐ Graphite or carbon paper
- ☐ Utility knife
- ☐ Scraps of colored tissue papers
- ☐ 10 small stickers
- ☐ Transparent tape

- ☐ Green and blue crayons
- ☐ White glitter
- ☐ Pie pan
- ☐ Bolts

- ☐ Glue stick
- ☐ Ruler

1 Make a stiff sheet of paper by gluing two sheets of green construction paper together with rubber cement. Make seven more stiff sheets.

2 Use the pencil to trace the large-tree and small-tree patterns from pages 26 and 27 onto tracing paper. Cut out the patterns.

3 Lay the patterns on the construction paper and draw around them. Draw five large and five small trees. Cut out the trees. Use the graphite or carbon paper to trace the flaps and the broken lines onto the trees.

4 **Have a parent cut the three slits for each flap using the utility knife and the ruler. Referring to the drawing, above, cut along the solid lines. Do not cut along the broken line.**

5 Gently push the flap away from you. Slide a piece of scrap paper *under* the tree but *over* the entire flap. Rub the four sides of the opening with the glue stick. Remove the scrap paper.

6 Fasten a square of tissue paper to the opening. (The side with the tissue is the back of the tree.)

7 Turn the tree over. Carefully lift the flap (do not crease at this time). Fasten a sticker to the tissue paper.

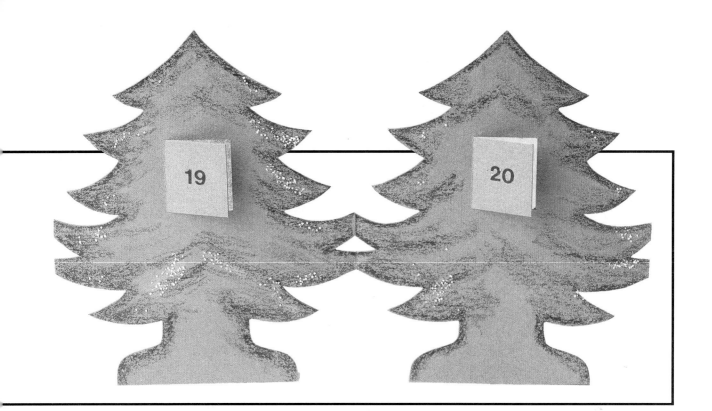

8 Use the green crayon to color along the tree edges and to draw branches. Use the blue crayon to outline the tree and to highlight the branches.

9 Using the glue stick, spread glue over the colored branches. Sprinkle glitter over the glue. With your fingers, push the glitter into the glue. Let the glue dry. Shake any extra glitter over the pie pan. Use this glitter on your next tree. Repeat steps 5–9 to make the remaining trees.

10 When all of your trees are completed, turn them over so the sides with the tissue paper are up. Tape the two widest branches of two large trees together. Cut away the tape that shows. Tape the three remaining large trees together in the same way. Repeat the same steps with first two, then three of the small trees.

11 Fold along the broken lines at the bottoms of the trees. To help the trees stand straight, place bolts on the tabs.

Advent Calendar

Make this row house to add twelve more days
to your Advent calendar.

Materials you will need to make the row house...

- [ ] Two sheets of 9x12-inch tan construction paper
- [ ] Rubber cement
- [ ] Pencil
- [ ] Tracing paper
- [ ] Scissors

- [ ] Scraps of colored tissue paper
- [ ] 12 small stickers
- [ ] Black ballpoint pen
- [ ] Bolts
- [ ] Scraps of red construction paper

- [ ] Graphite or carbon paper
- [ ] Utility knife
- [ ] Ruler
- [ ] Black felt-tip pen
- [ ] Glue stick

1 Glue the sheets of tan construction paper together with the rubber cement.

2 Use the pencil to trace the house pattern from page 28 onto tracing paper. Trace the roof trim, the door and window flaps, and the tab lines. Do not cut out the pattern.

3 Lay the graphite or carbon paper between the construction paper and the tracing paper. Trace over the traced lines to transfer the pattern to the tan paper. Trace all the house details, the window and door flaps, and the tab lines. Cut out the row house from the construction paper.

The difference between graphite and carbon papers...

Both of these papers have a coated side that transfers markings from one sheet of paper to another. Graphite paper is heavier and easier to use. And, when you use graphite paper, you can erase any mistakes you make as you trace your drawing. Both papers are available at crafts and art-supply stores.

4 Refer to Step 4 on page 20 to cut the window and door flaps.

5 Slip a piece of scrap paper under one of the window flaps. With the black felt-tip pen, outline the window flap. Repeat this step for all window and door flaps.

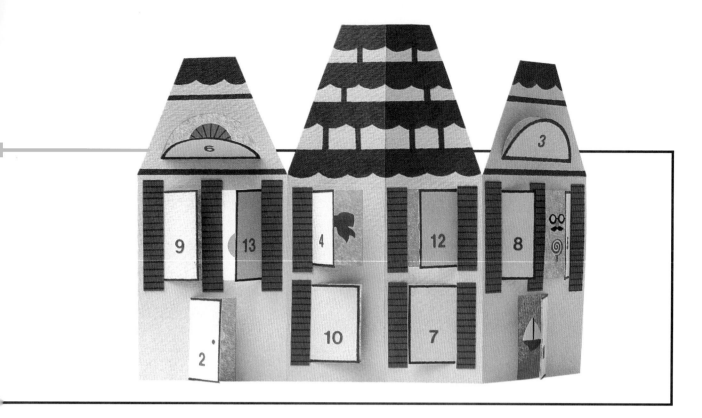

6 Color the roof trim with the felt-tip pen. To avoid making smudges on your house, begin coloring in the center of the house and work toward the edges.

7 Turn the house so the front is down. Referring to steps 5 and 6 on page 20, fasten the tissue squares to the window and door openings. Turn the house so the front is up. Fasten the stickers to the tissue squares.

8 With the ballpoint pen, draw lines evenly spaced across the red paper. Using the patterns on page 28, cut six large and six small shutters from this paper. Use the glue stick to fasten the shutters to the sides of the windows as shown in the photo, above.

9 Fold the house in half. Fold the tabs along the broken lines. Place bolts on the tabs to keep the house from tipping.

Advent Calendar

Complete your calendar by making the friendly snowmen,
the bright shining star, and the twig trees.

Materials you will need to make the snowmen, star, and trees...

- [ ] One sheet of 9x12-inch white construction paper
- [ ] Rubber cement
- [ ] Pencil
- [ ] Tracing paper
- [ ] Scissors
- [ ] Graphite or carbon paper
- [ ] Utility knife
- [ ] Ruler
- [ ] Glue stick
- [ ] Scraps of colored tissue paper
- [ ] Three small stickers
- [ ] Scraps of orange, yellow, and black construction paper
- [ ] Black ballpoint pen
- [ ] Wooden skewer
- [ ] Transparent tape
- [ ] Bush twigs
- [ ] White latex paint
- [ ] Large candy gumdrops
- [ ] ¼-inch red vinyl adhesive numbers

To make the snowmen...

1 Cut the white construction paper in half. Glue the two pieces of paper together with the rubber cement.

2 Fold a piece of tracing paper in half. Place the fold of the tracing paper on the fold line of the snowman pattern on page 29. Use the pencil to trace the shape. Cut out the shape through both thicknesses of the paper. Do not cut along the fold. Unfold the pattern. Lay the pattern on top of the completed snowmen on page 29. Trace the eyes, mouths, and buttons of each snowman.

3 Lay the graphite or carbon paper between the white construction paper and the snowmen pattern. Trace over the traced lines of the snowmen to transfer the pattern to the white paper.

4 **Refer to Step 4 on page 20 to cut the three sides of each flap.**

5 Use the glue stick to fasten the tissue paper to the backs of the openings. Fasten the stickers to the tissue paper on the front side.

6 Trace the hat, scarf, nose, and arm patterns from page 29 onto tracing paper. Cut out these patterns.

7 Trace the scarf, hat, and arm patterns onto the black paper. Trace the nose pattern onto the orange paper. Cut out the shapes. Add carrot lines to the nose with the pen. Use the glue stick to fasten these pieces to the snowmen. Use the pen to draw mouths and color eyes and buttons. (You can use a paper punch to make large buttons.) Crease snowmen on fold line to stand.

To make the star...

1 Trace the star pattern from page 29 onto tracing paper. Cut out the shape.

2 Draw around the star shape on the white paper. Cut out the star.

3 Refer to Step 4 on page 20 to cut the three sides of the flap.

4 Glue tissue paper to the back of the opening. Turn the star over and fasten a sticker to the tissue.

5 Cut five narrow strips of the yellow paper, each about 1 inch long. Glue the strips to the back of the star.

6 Use transparent tape to fasten the back of the star to the top of the skewer. Insert the other end of the skewer into a gumdrop.

To make twig trees...

Paint the twigs with the latex paint. When the twigs are dry, stand them in gumdrops.

To finish the calendar...

When you've completed all of the sections of your calendar, fasten the red adhesive numbers to each of the flaps. You will need enough stickers to make the numbers 1 through 25. Then, beginning the first day of December, fold back the flaps in their numbered sequence, one flap each day. Fold the flaps along the broken lines and make sharp creases to hold the flaps open.

Advent Calendar

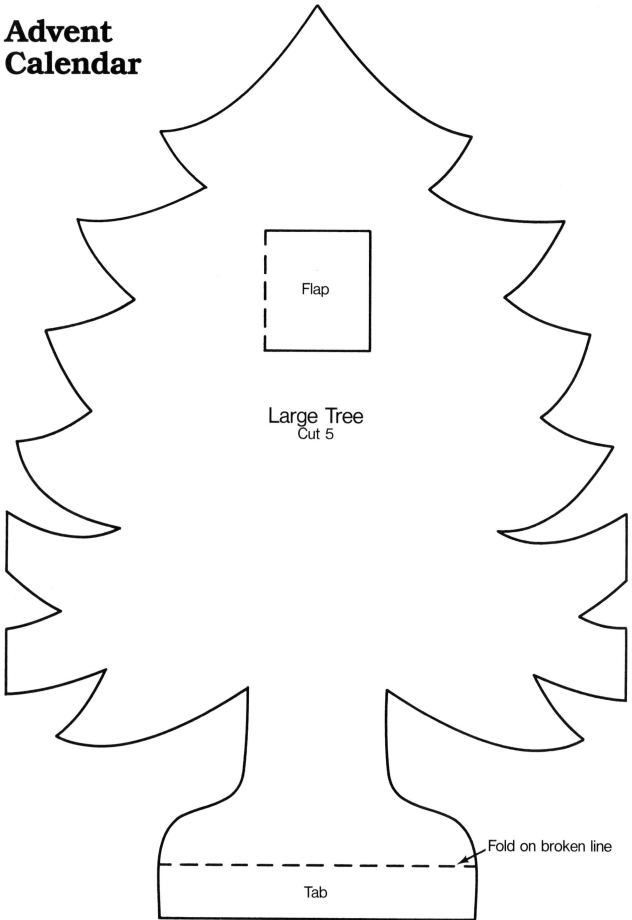

Flap

Large Tree
Cut 5

Fold on broken line

Tab

Use your school photos...

Use the small-tree pattern to make a card sure to be your grandparents' favorite. Begin by placing the pattern on a piece of folded construction paper. The straight edges of the two tree branches on the left side of the pattern should rest on the construction-paper fold. Trace around the shape. Then cut out the tree and cut off the tab along the bottom edge. Do not cut along the tree edges that are on the fold.

Cut out an opening to fit the size of one of your school photographs. Glue the photo to the back side of the opening. Decorate your card as you wish and write a merry greeting inside.

Try this...

Instead of using stickers, cut small designs from old Christmas cards or magazines and glue them to the tissue-paper squares on your Advent calendar. You might even write the numbers on the flaps with a red felt-tip pen instead of using the vinyl numbers. Go over the numbers several times with the pen so the numbers are clear.

Or, place these Advent-calendar projects on the gingerbread-house landscape from pages 52 and 53. Just skip the row house and make twelve more trees or stars to take the place of the flaps on the house.

Flap

Small Tree
Cut 5

Fold on broken line

Tab

Advent Calendar

House Shutter

Cut 6

Cut 6

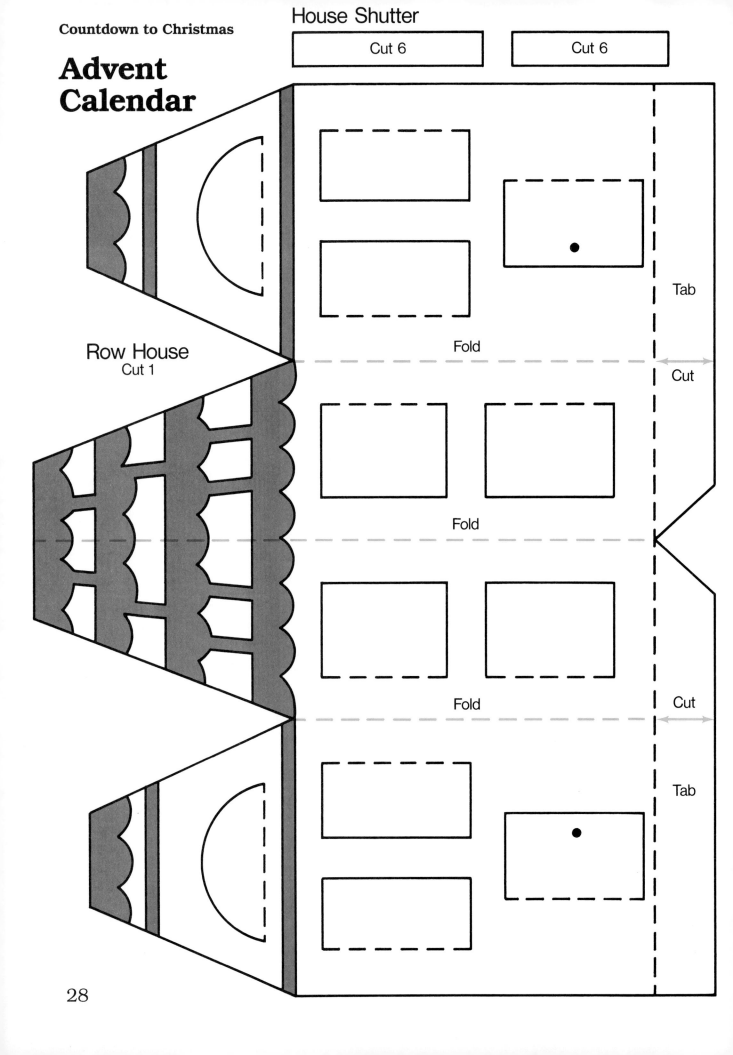

Tab

Fold

Cut

Row House
Cut 1

Fold

Fold

Cut

Tab

28

Mr. Snowman

Mrs. Snowman

Snowman

Hat
Cut 1

Arm
Cut 2

Nose
Cut 2

Scarf
Cut 1

Flap

Place
blue line
on fold of
tracing
paper

Star

29

Have a Merry, Beary Christmas

Here are three terrific projects that your parents would love to show off! The clay-pot bells look great on a front door. And the felt holly-leaf candle wreath, trimmed with the jolly bears, makes a perfect tabletop centerpiece.

Holly Advent Wreath

Cover a plastic-foam ring with lots of felt holly leaves. Tie ribbon bows around the bases of the candles for an added touch.

Materials you will need...

- ☐ 12-inch-diameter plastic-foam ring (2 inches wide)
- ☐ 1 roll of green party-streamer crepe paper
- ☐ Straight pins
- ☐ Large piece of paper

- ☐ Four red candles
- ☐ 1½ yards of ¼-inch red satin ribbon
- ☐ Crafts glue
- ☐ Tracing paper
- ☐ Paring knife

- ☐ Eight pieces of 9x12-inch kelly green felt
- ☐ Two pieces of 9x12-inch dark green felt
- ☐ Cotton balls
- ☐ ¼-inch red pom-poms

- ☐ Pencil
- ☐ Scissors

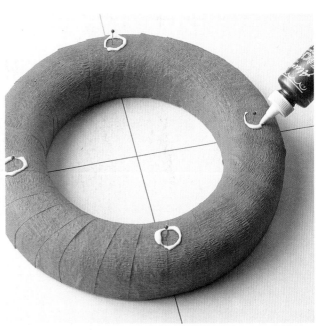

1 Wrap the crepe paper around the ring. Overlap the paper edges as you wrap. Hold the ends of the paper in place with straight pins.

To celebrate Advent, light one candle on the first Sunday of the season. Light two candles on the second Sunday. Continue to burn one additional candle on each of the next two Sundays.

2 Draw two perpendicular lines (a plus sign) through the center of the large piece of paper. Lay the ring on top of the paper so its center opening matches the point where the two lines intersect. Using the lines as guides, place four straight pins in the top of the ring to mark the positions for the candles. Run glue in a circle around each pin. Let the glue dry. Remove the pins.

3 Have a parent use the knife to scoop out a little of the plastic foam inside each of the four glue circles.

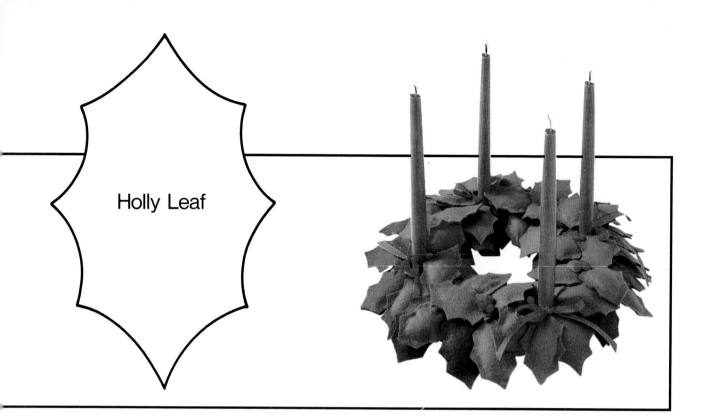

Holly Leaf

4 Trace the pattern for the holly leaf, above, onto tracing paper. Cut out the pattern. Lay the pattern on two thicknesses of felt and cut the holly leaves in pairs. Pin the pairs together until you are ready to assemble them. Cut 44 pairs of kelly green leaves and 11 pairs of dark green leaves.

Run glue just inside the edge of one leaf. Place a cotton ball in the center of the leaf. Lay another leaf on top of the cotton ball and pinch the edges of the two leaves. Repeat this step to make all of the leaves.

5 Use straight pins to fasten the leaves to the ring. When all of the leaves are pinned in place, glue red pom-poms to the leaves to cover any pins that show. Twist the candles into the four openings. Cut the ribbon into four equal pieces. Tie bows around each candle.

Cinnamon Bears

Cover plastic-foam balls with cinnamon and
sugar to make these festive bears.

Materials you will need to make one bear...

- ☐ Two 1½-inch-
  diameter plastic-
  foam balls

- ☐ 6 tiny plastic-
  foam eggs

- ☐ 3 straight pins with
  black-bead heads

- ☐ Pencil with eraser

- ☐ 2 teaspoons
  of sugar

- ☐ 2 teaspoons
  of cinnamon

- ☐ 10 inches of
  ⅛-inch-wide ribbon

- ☐ Waxed paper

- ☐ Paring knife

- ☐ Crafts glue

- ☐ Spice shaker

- ☐ Toothpicks

- ☐ Scissors

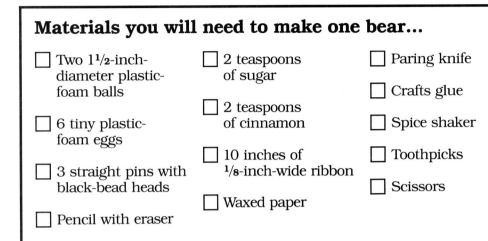

1 **Have a parent use the paring knife to
cut the plastic-foam pieces as shown in
the drawing above.** Cut away one rounded
edge of one 1½-inch plastic-foam ball for the
body of the bear. Cut away the narrow tips
from two of the eggs for the arms. Cut away
both ends of two eggs for the legs. Cut away
two-thirds of two of the eggs for the ears.

2 Use a pencil eraser to indent the center
of each ear. With the scissors, trim the
plastic foam as shown in the drawing below
so the ears will fit the curve of the head.
Glue the ears to the top of the head. Hold the
ears in place until the glue sets.

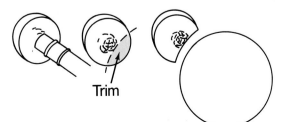

You can make tree ornaments...

For a tree ornament, glue the ends of a staple to the top of the bear's head. When the glue is dry, slip a ribbon through the staple and tie the ends. Break off the end of the toothpick that sticks out from the bottom of the body.

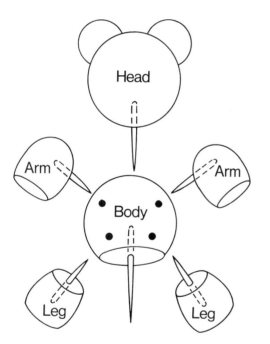

3 Put glue on one tip of each of six toothpicks. Using the drawing above as a guide, push one glued end of each pick into the arms, legs, head, and body. Do not assemble the bear at this time.

4 Mix the sugar and cinnamon in the spice shaker.

5 Holding the body piece by the toothpick, squeeze glue all around. With another toothpick, spread the glue around to cover the entire area.

Turn the page to finish the bears.

Cinnamon Bears

continued

To trim the wreath...

Push the toothpick at the bottom of the bear's body into the wreath next to a candle. Make three more bears to complete the bear decorations for the Advent wreath.

Make sweet scented bears...

Use potpourri instead of the cinnamon and sugar mixture to cover the bear as shown in Step 6, below. Potpourri is a sweet fragrant mixture of dried flower petals with spices. It can be purchased at crafts-supply stores and gift shops.

6 Sprinkle the cinnamon and sugar mixture over the entire body. Set the body on a piece of waxed paper to dry. Repeat steps 5 and 6 with all of the remaining portions of the bear.

7 When all of the pieces are dry, break off the ends of the toothpicks in the arms, legs, and head to within ½ inch of the foam. Do not break the end of the body toothpick.

8 Put glue on the end of the head toothpick. Push the head toothpick into the top of the body. Put glue on the ends of the arms and legs toothpicks. Using the dots on the drawing above Step 3 on page 35 as a guide, position the arms and legs in place on the body.

9 Push the black-bead straight pins into the head for the eyes and nose. Tie the ribbon in a bow around the bear's neck.

Clay-Pot Bells

Add ribbons and jingle bells to purchased clay pots to ring in the Christmas season.

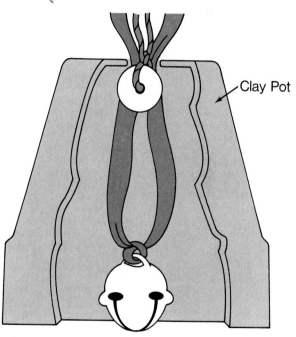

Materials you will need to make three bells...

- [ ] Two 2½-inch-diameter clay pots
- [ ] One 3-inch-diameter clay pot
- [ ] Three ¾-inch-diameter bells
- [ ] Toothpick
- [ ] Three 12½-millimeter wood beads
- [ ] 2 yards of ¼-inch-wide red ribbon
- [ ] 6 yards of red string
- [ ] Scissors

1 Cut the string and the ribbon into three equal lengths. You should have three string pieces that are 2 yards long and three ribbon pieces that are 24 inches long.

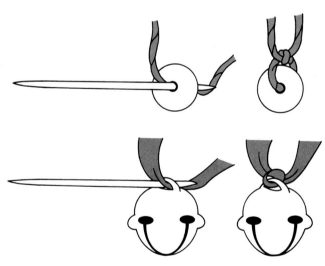

2 Use the toothpick to guide a string piece through each bead. Use the toothpick to guide a ribbon piece through the top of each bell. Center the beads and bells in the middle of the strings and the ribbons. Tie the strings and ribbons to hold the beads and bells in place.

Clay Pot

3 From the inside, draw one doubled string piece through the bottom hole of each pot. Draw the string pieces until the beads rest against the bottom holes. Leave enough string to hang the pots in a window, on a door, or in the center of an evergreen wreath or bough.

4 Push the beads aside and thread the ribbon ends through the bottom holes of the pots. Leave enough ribbon inside the pots for the bells to hang just below the rims. Tie the ribbons into bows.

37

Wrap
A
Special
Package

Tuck your Christmas
presents into bags you
make yourself. Use
wallpaper scraps or other
kinds of colorful papers.
Then trim the bags with
pinwheel bows,
candy canes, or other
project decorations
from this book.

Gift Bags

If the Japanese art of paper folding delights you, then you'll have no problem creating enough of these bags to hide all of your gifts.

Materials you will need to make the middle-size bag...

- [ ] 11x18-inch piece of wallpaper
- [ ] Ruler
- [ ] Pencil
- [ ] Glue stick
- [ ] Paper punch
- [ ] Gift-wrap yarn
- [ ] Scissors

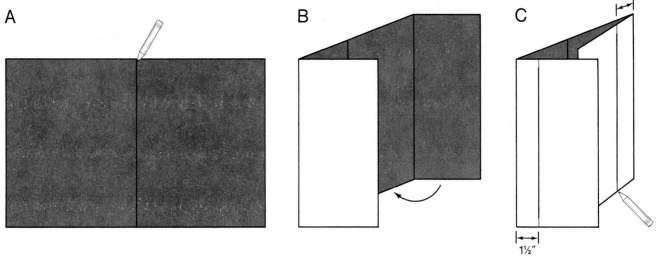

A   B   C

1 With the printed side of the wallpaper facing you, use the ruler and pencil to lightly draw a line down the center of the paper. See Drawing A.

2 Again with the printed side facing you, fold one edge of the paper to the centerline. Fold the other edge so it overlaps the first edge by 1 inch. Make sharp creases along the folds. See Drawing B.

3 Referring to Drawing C, use the ruler and pencil to draw a line 1½ inches in from each of the folds. With the scissors, cut ¼-inch slits through both thicknesses of the paper at the tops and bottoms of these drawn lines. You will make 4 small slits.

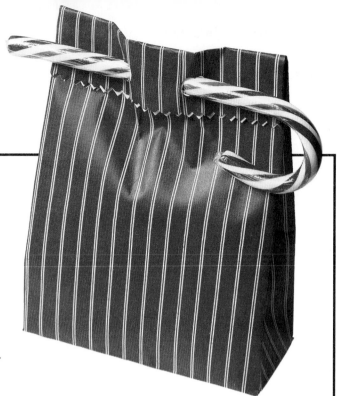

To make the small bag...

Use an 8½x12-inch piece of wallpaper. In Step 3, draw the lines and cut the slits 1 inch in from the folds. In Step 6, draw the line 1½ inches from one of the narrow edges. Cut 1½-inch corner slits in Step 7.

To make the large bag...

Use a 14x20-inch piece of wallpaper. In Step 3, draw the lines and cut the slits 2 inches from the folds. In Step 6, draw the line 2½ inches from one of the narrow edges. Cut 2½-inch corner slits in Step 7.

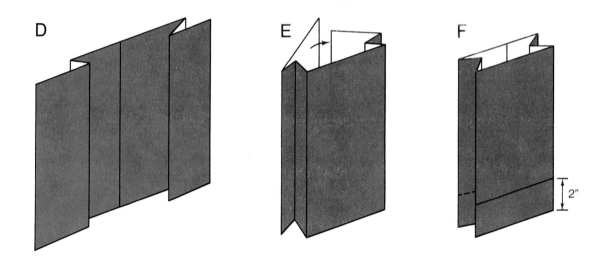

4 Using the slits as a guide and referring to Drawing D, fold back both flaps. Crease the folded edges.

5 Using the slits as a guide and referring to Drawing E, fold both flaps to the center of the unprinted side of the wallpaper. Overlap the edges. Use the glue stick to fasten the edges. Erase the pencil line on the printed side of the wallpaper.

6 To make the bottom of the bag, draw a line 2 inches from one of the narrow edges. See Drawing F. Fold all thicknesses of the paper along this line and make a crease. Unfold, then fold and crease the paper in the other direction. Unfold, then run your hand through the inside of the bag.

Turn the page to finish the bags.

Gift Bags

continued

Use other ideas in this book to decorate your bags...

To add a festive touch to your gift bags, attach paper soldiers (the patterns are on page 8) colored with felt-tip markers and spruced up with sequins. Or tie paper-animal ornaments (the patterns are on page 50) to your bags. You can even slip a candy cane through the two punched holes to hold the bag closed. And for more paper-folding fun, decorate your bags with the pinwheel bows shown on the opposite page.

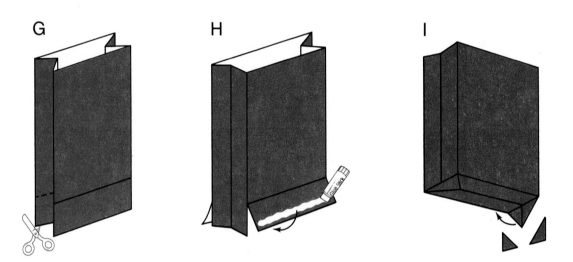

G   H   I

7 Using the folded lines you made in Step 6 on page 41 as a guide, cut 2-inch slits in each of the four corners. See Drawing G.

8 Run the glue stick across one of the long edges at the bottom of the bag. Overlap the two long edges ½ inch. Press them together. See Drawing H.

9 Referring to Drawing I, cut the short edges so they come to points in their centers. Rub the glue stick on the insides of these edges. Press these edges to the bottom of the bag.

10 Use the paper punch to punch two holes through all thicknesses at the top of the bag. Thread with gift-wrap yarn. Tie in a bow. Trim the bag as you wish.

Pinwheel Bows

Decorate packages with pinwheel bows made from Christmas wrapping papers.

Materials you will need...

- [ ] Scraps of wrapping papers
- [ ] Ruler
- [ ] Scissors
- [ ] Pencil
- [ ] Glue stick
- [ ] Nickel coin

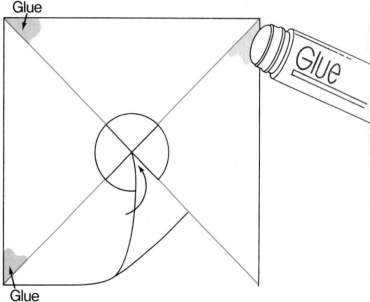

Glue

Glue

Glue

1 Rub the glue stick on the unprinted side of a square of wrapping paper. Glue this square to the unprinted side of a slightly larger piece of wrapping paper.

With the ruler and pencil, draw a square inside the smaller piece of paper. Draw two diagonal lines across the square to make one large X. Cut out the square.

2 Lay the coin in the center of the X where the two lines intersect. Draw around the coin. Using the blue lines in the drawing above as a guide, cut four diagonal lines.

3 Dab glue onto one of the two points at each slit. Bring one of these glued points to the center and fasten it in place. Working around the square, continue to lift and take each glued point to the center. With your finger, hold the points in the center until the glue sets. Add more glue, if necessary.

To make large pinwheels, draw and cut 5-inch squares. For small pinwheels, draw and cut 3- or 4-inch squares.

43

Easy Trims To Paint, Glue, Or Sew

To decorate and make the
merriest of trees, paint
purchased wood shapes,
assemble animal critters
from wallpaper scraps,
and trim vine wreaths
with buttons and bows.

Paper-Animal Ornaments

Wallpaper scraps and buttons are all you
need to make these playful creature decorations.

Materials you will need...

- ☐ Print-wallpaper scraps
- ☐ ³/₈-inch-diameter shirt buttons
- ☐ Embroidery floss or other sewing threads that match wallpaper colors
- ☐ Colored markers
- ☐ Green carpet thread
- ☐ Scraps of felt (for bunny and bear scarves)
- ☐ Scraps of ¹/₄-inch-wide ribbon (for cat bow)
- ☐ Glue stick
- ☐ Sewing needle
- ☐ Scissors
- ☐ Tracing paper
- ☐ No. 2 soft-lead pencil

1 Select an animal pattern from page 50. Use a pencil to trace onto tracing paper the patterns for the body and the movable arms, legs, or tail. Trace the details of the face and the dots that mark the placement of the buttons. Cut out the patterns.

2 Cut the wallpaper scraps into 6-inch squares. Using the glue stick, cover the back of one square of wallpaper with glue. Fasten the back of another wallpaper square to the first piece.

If you don't have scraps of wallpaper at your house, visit a wallpaper store and ask about their out-of-date sample books. Most stores give away or charge a small amount for these books.

3 Trace the outlines of the animal patterns onto the wallpaper. Follow the directions on page 50 to determine the number of pieces to trace.

4 Referring to Step 1 on page 48, make your own carbon paper on the back of your tracing pattern. Use this carbon paper to transfer the face and all other markings to the wallpaper pieces.

5 With scissors, cut out the wallpaper shapes. Use the needle to punch holes through the dots on the shapes.

6 Thread the needle with double strands of thread that match the wallpaper. Knot the strands about 2 inches from the end.

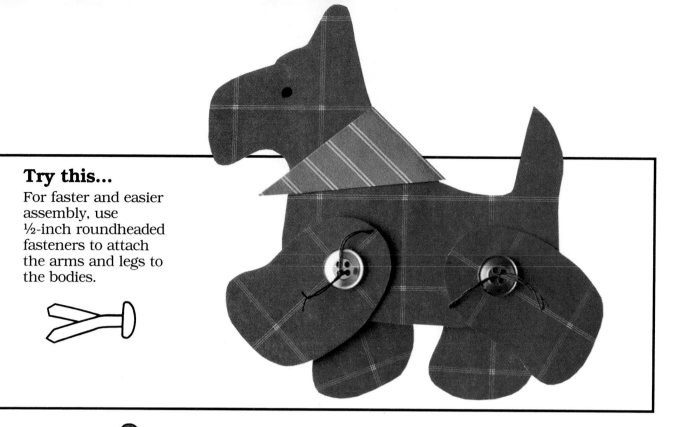

Try this...

For faster and easier
assembly, use
½-inch roundheaded
fasteners to attach
the arms and legs to
the bodies.

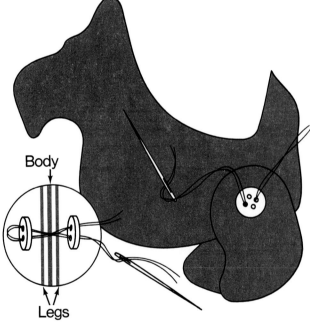

Body

Legs

7 Match the dots on *each* body part to the
dots on the body. Using the directions
that follow, sew one button to *each* side of
the animal to attach the movable parts: Sew
through the button, into the arm or leg,
through the body, through the arm or leg on
the other side, then through another button.
Then push the threaded needle back
through the body parts and the two buttons.
Knot the ends of the thread. Trim the thread
ends to leave 1-inch strands. Repeat this step
with the remaining body parts.

8 With the markers, draw the details of
the face on both sides of the animal. Cut
a scarf from a wallpaper scrap. Glue the
scarf to the dog. Glue a ribbon bow to the cat
and tie felt scarves to the bunny and bear.

9 Thread the needle with a 10-inch piece
of the carpet thread. Draw the threaded
needle through the dot for the hanger.
Remove the needle and knot the ends of the
thread together to make a loop for hanging
the ornament.

47

Wooden Ornaments

Use colored pens to decorate lots of precut wooden tree ornaments that you can buy in crafts stores.

Materials you will need...

- ☐ Purchased wooden tree ornaments (available at crafts-supply stores)
- ☐ Spray varnish
- ☐ Red, green, and brown felt-tip calligraphy pens
- ☐ Tracing paper
- ☐ No. 2 soft-lead pencil

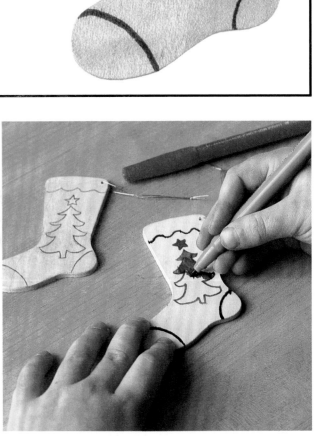

1 Buy wooden ornaments that match the patterns on page 51. With a pencil, trace the patterns onto tracing paper. To make your own carbon paper, turn the tissue patterns over and color only on top of the design lines with the No. 2 soft-lead pencil. (Do not color the outline shapes.) With the colored sides down, center and lay the traced patterns onto the wooden ornaments. Trace over the designs to transfer the markings to the wood. Remove the patterns.

2 Draw over the design lines with the brown pen. Color the ornaments with the red or green pens. Spray the ornaments with the varnish. Hang them in an open space to dry.

If you can't find wooden shapes that match the designs that we used, choose other shapes that are available in crafts stores. You easily can draw and color your own designs on these shapes.

48

Vine-Wreath Ornaments

Glue colorful buttons and tie ribbon bows on tiny vine wreaths to trim your tree.

Materials you will need to make one ornament...

- ☐ Purchased 4-inch-diameter vine wreath (available at crafts-supply stores)
- ☐ One yard each of ¼-inch-wide red and green ribbons
- ☐ Assorted shapes and sizes of red, green, and white buttons
- ☐ Crafts glue
- ☐ Green carpet thread
- ☐ Scissors

1 Put a dab of glue on the backs of the buttons. Fasten the buttons to the wreath, spacing them about 1 inch apart. You can glue tiny white buttons on top of some or all of the red and green buttons.

2 Leaving a 7-inch-long tail at the start, wrap the red ribbon around the wreath. Let the ribbon lie between the buttons as you wrap it. Then tie the ribbon ends.

3 Leaving a 7-inch-long tail at the start, wrap the green ribbon around the wreath in the opposite direction. Let the green ribbon overlap the red ribbon to form Xs between the buttons. Tie the green-ribbon ends.

4 Hold the ends of the red and green ribbons together and tie them into one bow. Loop an 11-inch-long green thread around the top of the wreath. Knot the ends to make a loop for hanging.

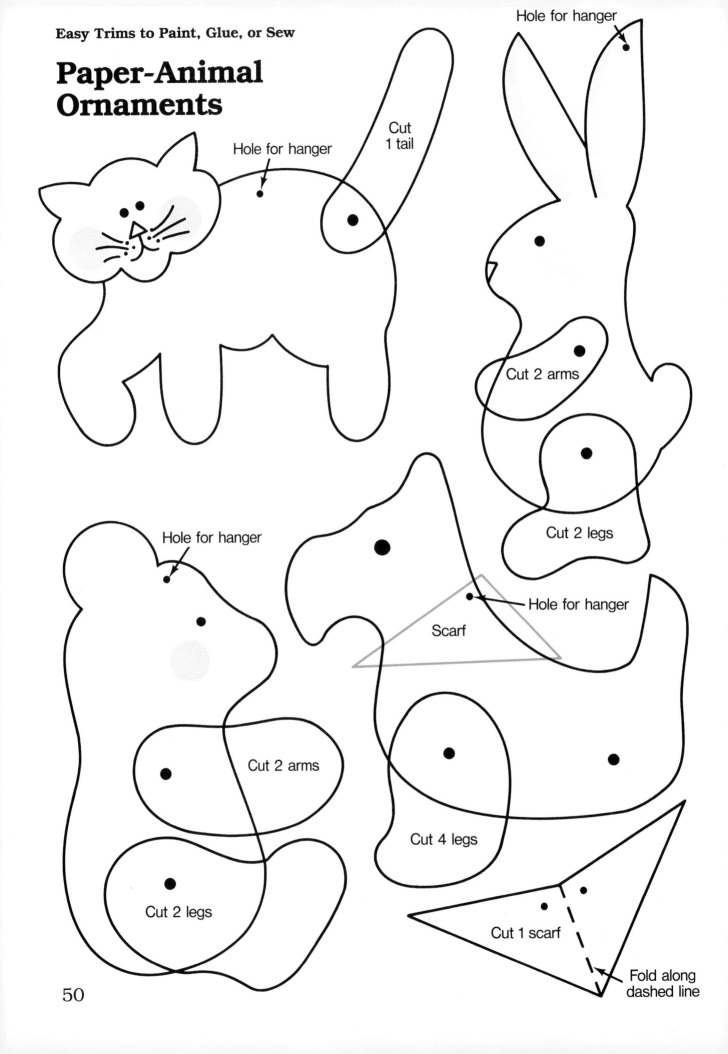

Easy Trims to Paint, Glue, or Sew

Paper-Animal Ornaments

Hole for hanger

Cut 1 tail

Hole for hanger

Cut 2 arms

Cut 2 legs

Hole for hanger

Scarf

Hole for hanger

Cut 2 arms

Cut 4 legs

Cut 2 legs

Cut 1 scarf

Fold along dashed line

50

Wooden Ornaments

Fun to Make, Fun to Eat

Gather your family to make a candy house that sits in a snowy scene. Gumdrops, candy canes, pretzels, graham crackers, ice-cream cones, marshmallows, hard candies, and frosting all combine to bring a cardboard house to life.

No-Bake Candy House

Let your parents or older brother or sister assemble
the frame of your house from a cardboard box.

Materials you will need to assemble the house frame...

☐ Cardboard box
  approximately
  10½x13 inches and
  18 inches tall

☐ Pencil

☐ Ruler

☐ Utility knife

☐ Duct tape

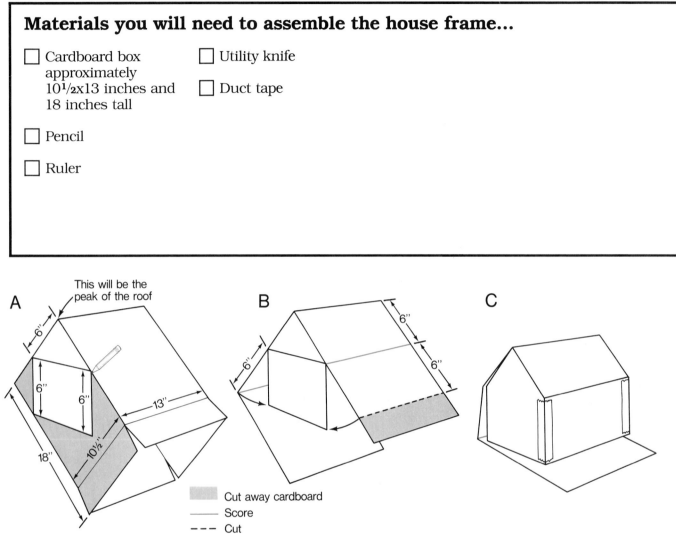

This will be the peak of the roof

A   B   C

6"   6"   6"   6"   6"

13"

18"   10½"

▨ Cut away cardboard
— Score
--- Cut

1 **Note: The frame of the house should be built by a parent or an older teenager.** Standing at a table, lay the box on one of its narrow sides so that the bottom faces away from you. Referring to Drawing A, mark 6 inches from both sides of one corner on the side facing you. Draw a line to connect these two points. Then, from the two points, draw two 6-inch lines perpendicular to the line you just drew. Draw a line to connect the ends of these two new lines.

Repeat this step on the opposite side of the box using the corresponding corner.

2 Use the utility knife to cut away the portion of the box that is shaded blue on Drawing A. Do the same on the opposite side of the box. The two narrow sides of the house and its roof peak are now established.

3 Referring to Drawing B, draw a straight line 6 inches below, and parallel to, the roof peak on both of the long sides of the box. Use the utility knife to score these lines. Fold along the scored lines so that the long sides meet the narrow sides. Cut away the excess cardboard from the shorter of the two long sides to match the base of the house. Use the duct tape to fasten this long side to the two narrow sides.

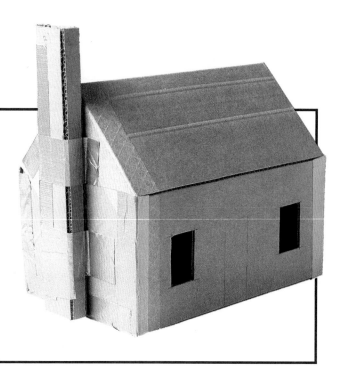

Use other box sizes...

You can cut frames for houses from all sizes of boxes following the directions below. For a larger box, use the same marking and cutting instructions. For a smaller box, change the 6-inch markings and cutting instructions in steps 1 and 3 to 4- or 5-inch dimensions. Adjust the door, window, and chimney measurements to conform to the new scale.

D   E   F

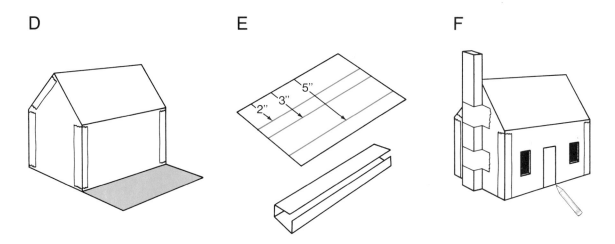

4 Referring to Drawing C, score the remaining long side along the base of the house. Fold along this score line and slide the cardboard under the house. Referring to Drawing D, tape the sides together and cut away the excess cardboard that extends from the base of the house. Tape the base edges.

5 To make the chimney, cut a piece of scrap cardboard to measure 6x13 inches. Referring to Drawing E, draw lines 2 inches, then 3 inches, then 5 inches from one of the long edges of the strip. Score these lines. Fold the cardboard along the scored lines and tape the edges together. Tape the chimney to one of the house's narrow sides as shown in Drawing F.

6 Referring to Drawing F, cut two 1½x2¼-inch windows on each of the house's long sides. Mark one 1½x4-inch door on one of the long sides. Make sure the tops of the windows are in line with the top of the door.

Turn the page to decorate the house.

No-Bake Candy House

You'll have tons of fun decorating your house
with colorful candies and lots of frosting.

Materials you will need to decorate the house...

- [ ] Three batches of frosting
- [ ] Spatula
- [ ] Tube of white frosting
- [ ] Vanilla-flavored candy coating
- [ ] Cinnamon-covered graham crackers
- [ ] Filled sugar wafers
- [ ] Small pretzels
- [ ] 5 or 6 bags of assorted candies
- [ ] Waxed paper

1 Following the recipe, opposite, make three batches of frosting. Use the spatula to spread frosting on one side of the house. Break the graham crackers into sections. Cover the frosted side of the house with the cracker sections. Continue around the house, frosting only one side at a time and covering the frosting with the cracker sections. Do not frost the triangular portions on the two narrow sides of the house at this time.

2 To make the shutters, decorate one side of eight sugar wafers with the tube frosting and small candies. Fasten the shutters to the house. For the sills, fasten candies to the bottoms of the windows.

For the door, use cracker sections and a sugar wafer cut in half. Decorate the two wafer pieces. Fasten the door pieces to the house. Outline the door with the tube frosting. Add a candy doorknob. Dip 15 pretzels into melted candy coating. Dry the pretzels on waxed paper. Fasten five pretzels above the windows and the door.

56

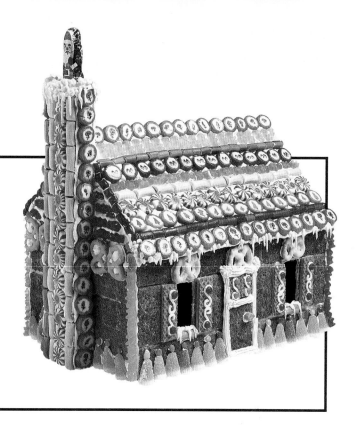

Frosting recipe for one batch...

3 egg whites, at room temperature
3 cups confectioners' sugar
½ teaspoon cream of tartar

Mix the egg whites, sugar, and cream of tartar in a small mixing bowl. Beat with an electric mixer on high speed until the frosting is stiff. Add more sugar, if necessary. Cover the frosting with a damp cloth and store in the refrigerator until you are ready to use it.

3 To make the overhangs on the long sides of the roof, fasten one row of cracker sections along each roof edge. The crackers should extend ½ inch beyond the edges. Then frost one side of the roof. Working from the bottom, add rows of candies to the roof. Then frost and decorate the other side of the roof.

Frost the two triangular portions on the narrow sides of the house. Cover with candies. Fasten the remaining candy-coated pretzels along the bottom edges of the triangular sections.

4 Frost the chimney and decorate with candies. Use the tube frosting to make the snow on top of the chimney. To make icicles, dribble short strips of tube frosting onto waxed paper and let dry. When dry, fasten the strips to the edges of the roof, the windowsills, and the chimney.

Decorate the bottom edges of the house with candy. If you use gumdrops, cut them in half before you fasten them to the house.

Turn the page to make the landscape trims.

No-Bake Candy House

Make a landscape from frosting and other treats
to create a winter wonderland for your candy house.

Materials you will need to make the landscape...

- ☐ Three batches of frosting (see recipe, page 57)
- ☐ Spatula
- ☐ Green and red paste food coloring
- ☐ Tube of white frosting
- ☐ Pretzel sticks
- ☐ Vanilla-flavored candy coating
- ☐ Aluminum foil
- ☐ Large piece of cardboard
- ☐ Empty margarine tubs
- ☐ Duct tape
- ☐ Waxed paper
- ☐ Large marshmallows
- ☐ Ice-cream cones
- ☐ Small candies
- ☐ Small candy canes
- ☐ Ribbon candy
- ☐ Toothpicks

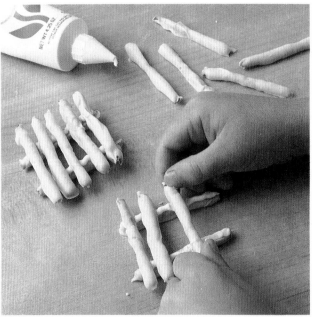

1 Use the ice-cream cones to make the trees. First, color two cups of frosting with green food coloring. Cover the cones with the green frosting. Then add small candies to decorate the trees. When the frosting on the trees is dry, dribble white frosting on the treetops to look like snow.

To make taller trees, put a dab of frosting on the tip of one cone and set a second cone on its top. Make lots of trees, but complete each one before going on to the next one. Set your trees on the frosted cardboard base.

2 To make the fencing, first melt and color two squares of the candy coating with red food coloring (to make it pink). Dip 30 pretzel sticks into the pink coating. Lay the pretzels on waxed paper to dry.

To make one fence unit, run a string of tube frosting down the middles of two coated pretzel sticks. With their frosted edges up, lay the two pretzels 1 inch apart. Lay pink pretzels on top of the frosted ones. Let the frosting dry. Make three more fence units. Use tube frosting to fasten the fences to the frosted cardboard base.

To make a base...

Find a large piece of cardboard. Fasten upside-down empty margarine tubs to it with duct tape. Fasten aluminum foil to the cardboard to create a lake. Spread two batches of frosting over the cardboard and tubs.

3 With the marshmallows, make shrubs to stand in front of the door. For best results, first leave the marshmallows out in the open for a couple of days. This makes their surfaces firmer and easier to work with. Poke a toothpick into one flat side of two firm marshmallows. Cover these two marshmallows with green frosting. Decorate them with small candies. Stick the ends of the toothpicks into undecorated marshmallows. Set the shrubs on the base.

4 For one sled, use two small candy canes and a piece of ribbon candy. Spread white frosting along one side of the ribbon candy. Hold the two candy canes about ½ inch apart and place the ribbon candy on top of the canes. Hold the sled in place until the frosting sets. Do not move the sled until the frosting dries. Repeat these steps to make more sleds. Set your sleds on the base.

Welcome Santa With Treats And Trims

Leave Santa goodies on a place mat and in a mug you've decorated just for him. He'll know you've been busy—and good— when he sees all the tree ornaments and the socks you've made, too.

Felt Tree Ornaments

Deck your tree with colorful felt tree ornaments
to get Santa's attention on Christmas Eve.

Materials you will need...

- ☐ 9x12-inch pieces of tan, red, white, and black felt
- ☐ 5-millimeter white pom-poms
- ☐ 7-millimeter red pom-poms
- ☐ Glue stick
- ☐ Extra-sticky crafts glue
- ☐ Tracing paper
- ☐ Pencil
- ☐ Paper punch
- ☐ Needle
- ☐ Green carpet thread
- ☐ Scissors
- ☐ Thin cardboard

1 Trace the outlines of the reindeer body and the antlers from page 68 onto tracing paper. Rub the glue stick over the back of the tracing paper. Fasten the tracing paper to the cardboard. Then cut out the pattern pieces.

2 Trace around the body pattern onto the tan felt. Trace around the antlers onto the white felt. Cut out the felt pieces. Use the paper punch to punch out a black-felt eye.

Try this...

If you don't have red or white pom-poms, use the paper punch to punch out the red-felt nose and the white-felt spots.

Add felt scarves...

The deer on Santa's place mat on page 60 have striped scarves. Use the pattern on page 68 to cut white felt scarves. Trim the scarves with strips of red felt. Glue the scarves to the deer's necks.

3 Cut a 4½x6-inch piece of red felt. Use the extra-sticky glue to fasten the body and antlers to the red felt. Make sure there is a narrow red border around *all* sides of the deer. Glue a red pom-pom in place for the nose. Glue the eye in place. Then glue five or six white pom-poms to the deer's back.

4 When the glue is dry, cut the deer from the red felt. Leave a narrow red border to outline the deer's shape. Thread a needle with a 12-inch length of carpet thread. Pull the thread through the top of the ornament. Knot the ends of the thread to make a loop for hanging the ornament. Repeat steps 1–4 to make additional ornaments.

On pages 68–69 you'll find patterns for other felt ornaments.

Christmas Stockings

Santa will get a kick out of this stocking
you make all by yourself.

Materials you will need...

- [ ] ½ yard of red-and white-checked flannel-backed vinyl
- [ ] ¾-inch self-adhesive red vinyl letters
- [ ] ¼-inch-diameter green macramé cord
- [ ] Straight pins

- [ ] Scissors
- [ ] Pencil
- [ ] Tracing paper
- [ ] Glue stick
- [ ] Large brown paper grocery sack

- [ ] Extra-sticky crafts glue
- [ ] Paper punch
- [ ] Transparent tape

 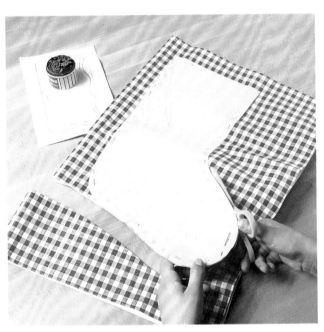

1 Trace the stocking patterns (foot and top) from pages 70–71 onto the tracing paper. Trace the lacing holes. Cut out the patterns. Cut the grocery sack apart so you have one large piece of paper. Rub the glue stick over the backs of the traced patterns. Fasten the patterns to the brown paper to make one sock pattern. Cut the pattern from the brown paper. Trace the cuff pattern from page 71 onto the tracing paper. Cut out the tissue cuff pattern.

2 Fold the vinyl in half with the flannel sides facing. Pin the stocking pattern to the vinyl. Cutting through the two thicknesses of the vinyl, cut out the stocking. Do not remove the pattern from the vinyl. Pin the cuff pattern to one thickness of the vinyl. Cut out the cuff.

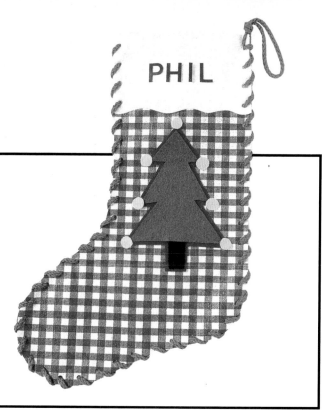

Decorate your stocking...

● Use the red vinyl letters to spell your name on the cuff of your sock.

● Fasten a felt ornament like the ones shown on pages 60–61 to your stocking. Refer to pages 62–63 for the felt-ornament directions and pages 68–69 for the patterns.

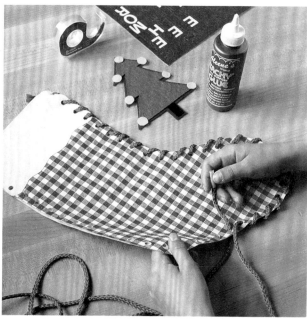

3 Use the paper punch to punch out the lacing holes around the stocking. Punch through both the pattern and the two thicknesses of the vinyl. When all the holes are punched, remove the pattern.

4 Put several dabs of the extra-sticky glue in the center of the vinyl side of the cuff. Fasten the cuff to one side of the stocking. This is the front. When the glue is dry, turn the stocking so its back is up. Punch holes through the cuff using the holes that are already punched as guides.

5 Cut a 2¼-yard length of macramé cord. Knot one end of the cord. Wrap the other end with tape. From the back of the sock, push the taped end through the top lacing hole on the *toe* side of the sock. Pull the cord until the knot rests against the lacing hole. Take the cord to the back of the sock and thread it through the next hole. Lace the sock in this manner. When the lacing is completed, knot the cord to make a loop for hanging. Slip the remaining cord under two inches of the lacings on the back. Cut the excess cord. Glue the cord end to the sock.

Santa's Place Mat and Mug

Use the reindeer ornament or any of the other felt tree ornaments
to decorate a place mat and mug for Santa's snacks.

Materials you will need...

- ☐ Paper punch
- ☐ 14x20-inch piece of red-and-white-checked flannel-backed vinyl
- ☐ Masking tape
- ☐ Transparent tape
- ☐ Scissors
- ☐ 3½ yards of ¼-inch-diameter green macramé cord
- ☐ 30 inches of ⅛-inch-diameter green macramé cord
- ☐ Pencil
- ☐ Extra-sticky glue
- ☐ Scraps of red and white felt
- ☐ Tracing paper
- ☐ Purchased mug

To make the place mat...

1 Place the vinyl piece so the vinyl side is up. Fold under each of the four sides about 1 inch. Crease the folds. Place small pieces of masking tape on the flannel side to temporarily hold the folds in place.

2 Use the paper punch to punch holes through both thicknesses of the vinyl. Space the holes 1 inch apart and ¼ inch away from the folds.

3 Knot one end of the ¼-inch-diameter macramé cord. Tape the other end with a strip of transparent tape (to look like the end of a shoelace).

4 From the flannel side of the mat, push the taped end of the cord through one of the lacing holes. Pull the cord until the knot rests against the hole. Take the cord to the flannel side of the mat and thread it through the next lacing hole. Continue to lace the mat in this manner. When the lacing is completed, slip the end of the cord under two inches of the lacings on the flannel side of the mat. Trim the excess cord. Glue the end of the cord to the mat.

5 To decorate the mat as shown opposite, make three reindeer ornaments following the directions on pages 62–63. Referring to the photograph on the opposite page, glue the deer to the vinyl side of the mat. Use the ⅛-inch-diameter cord to make the reins as follows: Glue one end under the scarf of the reindeer on the left side. Drape the cord to the center deer, and then to the last deer. Glue the cord under each scarf. Take the remaining cord to the back side through a lacing hole. Trim the excess cord. Glue the end of the cord to the mat.

To make the mug...

1 Trace the top candy cane in the drawing at right onto tracing paper. Cut out the pattern.

2 Draw around the pattern onto the white felt. Draw two candy-cane shapes. Cut out the shapes. Glue narrow strips of red felt on top of the white felt to create the striping.

3 Using the drawing at right as a guide, glue the canes to a piece of red felt. When the glue is dry, cut the shape from the red felt. Leave a narrow red border to outline the shape. Glue the decoration on one side of the mug. Using an 8-inch piece of macramé cord or ribbon, tie a bow through the handle.

Mug Pattern

Felt Tree Ornaments

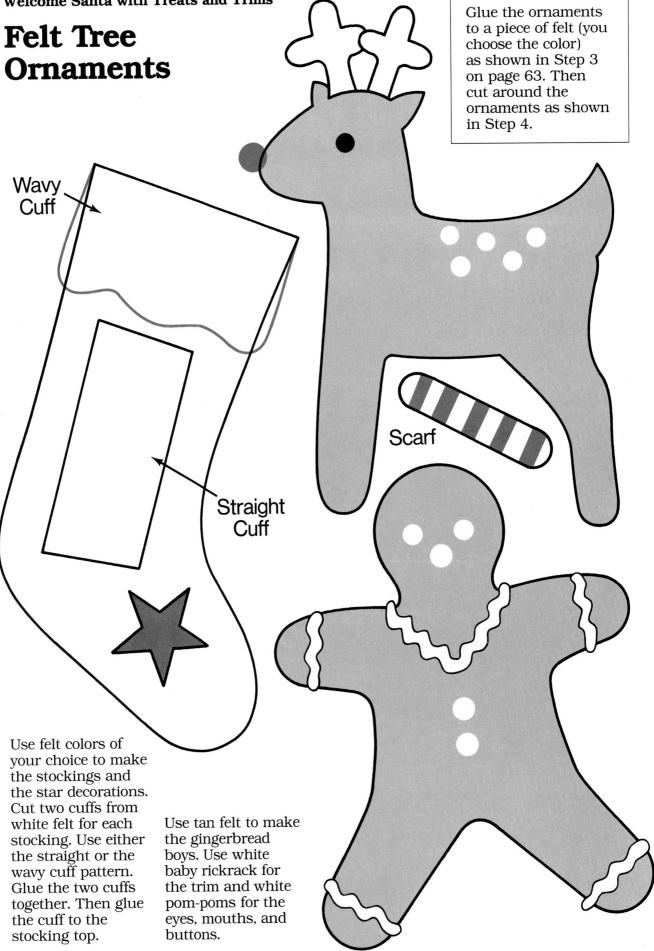

Glue the ornaments to a piece of felt (you choose the color) as shown in Step 3 on page 63. Then cut around the ornaments as shown in Step 4.

Wavy Cuff

Straight Cuff

Scarf

Use felt colors of your choice to make the stockings and the star decorations. Cut two cuffs from white felt for each stocking. Use either the straight or the wavy cuff pattern. Glue the two cuffs together. Then glue the cuff to the stocking top.

Use tan felt to make the gingerbread boys. Use white baby rickrack for the trim and white pom-poms for the eyes, mouths, and buttons.

Use green felt to make the trees and black felt to make the trunks. Glue red pom-poms to the branches after the trees have been cut from the felt backing pieces.

Use tan felt for the lollipop sticks. Use a felt color of your choice for each candy circle. Cut the swirl from the white felt and glue it to the candy circle.

Use felt colors of your choice to make the stars.

Use white felt to make the whole candy canes. Then, for the stripes, glue narrow strips of red felt to the white felt.

69

Christmas Stockings

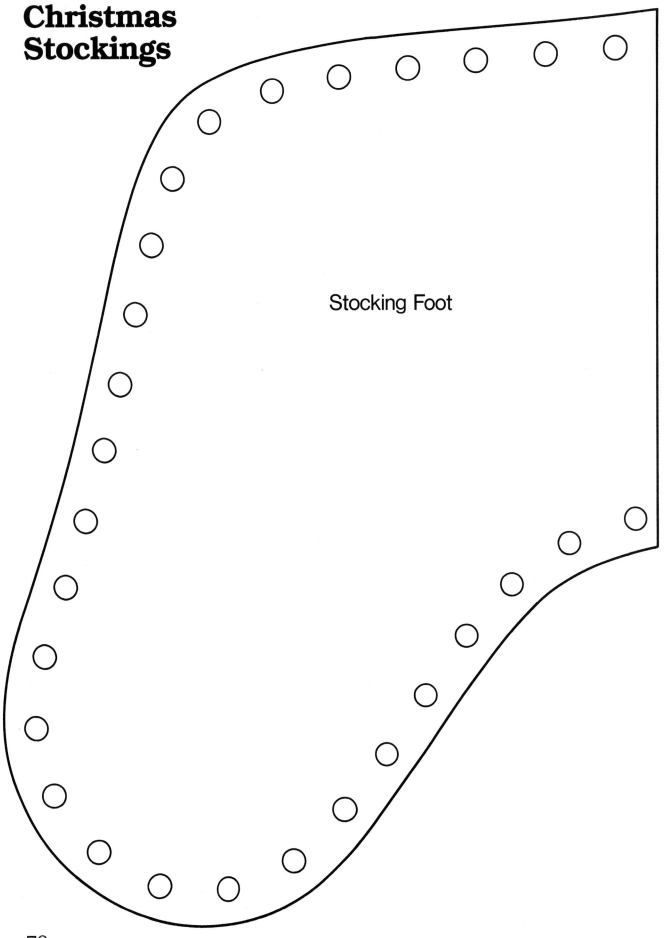

Stocking Foot

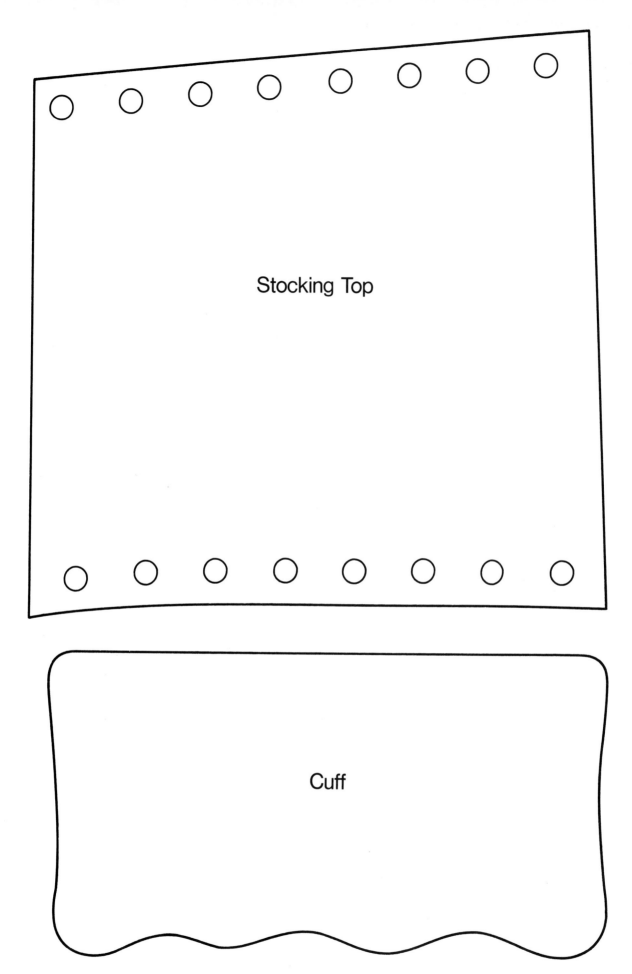

Stocking Top

Cuff

Cut Snowflakes For Holiday Decorating

Cut perfect paper snowflakes by following our diagrams on page 78. Then use the flakes to decorate place mats, coasters, napkin rings, and even a wreath. Or punch a snowflake design into a tin can to make a candle holder.

Party-Table Toppers

Make your own place mats, coasters, and napkin rings. Then decorate them with crisp white snowflakes for a dazzling Christmas party.

Materials you will need...

- [ ] Blue poster board
- [ ] Tracing paper
- [ ] Carbon or graphite paper
- [ ] Typing paper
- [ ] Pencil
- [ ] Scissors
- [ ] Glue stick
- [ ] Pizza pan
- [ ] Cup
- [ ] Clear adhesive-backed vinyl

To make a napkin ring...

1 Trace the napkin-ring pattern from page 79 onto tracing paper. Cut out the pattern. Trace around the pattern onto the blue poster board. Use the carbon paper to transfer the slit markings on the tissue pattern to the poster board. Cut out the shape. Do not cut the slits.

2 Fold a 2½-inch square of typing paper according to the instructions on page 78. Cut a snowflake from the folded paper. Dab glue onto one side of the snowflake. Fasten the snowflake to the circle of the napkin ring. Use only enough glue to hold the snowflake in place.

74

Snowflake sizes...

Small—Use 2½-inch squares of paper.
Medium—Use 3-inch squares of paper.
Large—Use 6-inch squares of paper.

To make a place mat...

1 Use a pizza pan or a canning-kettle lid as your pattern. Draw around the pan or lid onto the poster board. Cut out the mat.

2 Using the instructions on page 78, make large, medium, and small snowflakes.

3 Have fun arranging your snowflakes on the mat. When you like your arrangement, pick up your snowflakes, one at a time, dab glue onto their backs, and fasten them in place.

4 Cut two pieces of adhesive-backed vinyl slightly larger than the mat. Fasten the vinyl to both sides of the mat. Trim the excess vinyl with the scissors.

3 Cut two pieces of adhesive-backed vinyl slightly larger than the napkin ring. Gradually remove the backing from one piece of the vinyl and, at the same time, fasten the sticky side to the front of the napkin ring.

Fasten another piece of adhesive-backed vinyl to the back of the napkin ring. Carefully trim the excess vinyl from around the napkin ring. Then cut the slits. Fold the ring around a napkin. Slip the slits inside each other to hold the napkin.

To make a coaster...

1 Use a 4-inch-diameter cup or jar lid as your pattern. Draw around the cup or lid onto the poster board. Cut out the coaster shape.

2 Use a 3-inch square of typing paper to make the snowflake for the coaster. Fasten it in place. Complete the coaster, referring to Step 4, above.

Wreath with Snowflake Trims

Cut snowflakes from origami papers
to decorate a purchased vine wreath

Materials you will need...

- [ ] Vine wreath, about 16 inches in diameter
- [ ] Blue poster board
- [ ] White spray paint
- [ ] Pencil, scissors
- [ ] Transparent tape
- [ ] Clear adhesive-backed vinyl
- [ ] Florist wire
- [ ] Glue stick
- [ ] Eight silver pipe cleaners
- [ ] Origami papers in assorted colors

1 Lightly spray the vine wreath with one coat of white paint. Set the wreath aside to dry.

2 Fold the origami papers according to the instructions on page 78. Cut lots of different-size snowflakes from assorted colors of the papers.

3 With the glue stick, fasten each snowflake to a piece of poster board slightly larger than the snowflake itself. Draw a hexagon (six-sided shape) around each snowflake onto the poster board. Cut out the hexagons.

4 Cut pieces of the adhesive-backed vinyl slightly larger than the hexagons. Remove the backing from the vinyl. Fasten the vinyl to the snowflake side of each hexagon. Cut away the excess vinyl.

5 To fasten one snowflake to the wreath, push a 6-inch length of florist wire around one of the vines of the wreath. Twist the wire close to the vine to hold it in place. Fasten the ends of the wire to the back of the hexagon with the transparent tape. Repeat this step to fasten all of the snowflakes to the wreath. Twist the wires so the snowflakes face forward.

6 To add sparkle to your wreath, center and twist the silver pipe cleaners around the vines of the wreath. Space the pipe cleaners in a pleasing arrangement around the wreath. Wrap the ends of the pipe cleaners around a pencil to curl them.

Tin-Can Candle Holders

Hammer snowflake designs into tin cans to make festive candle holders.

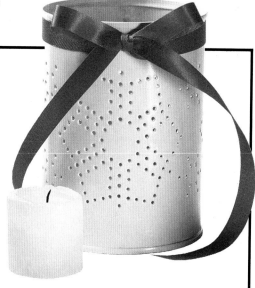

Materials you will need...

- [ ] 20-ounce tin can without ridges
- [ ] ½-inch-wide blue satin ribbon
- [ ] Gloss white enamel spray paint
- [ ] Hammer and nail
- [ ] Spray primer
- [ ] Two rubber bands
- [ ] Towel
- [ ] Tracing paper
- [ ] Transparent tape
- [ ] Pencil, scissors
- [ ] Votive candle

Use pineapple cans...

This project requires a tin can without ridges on its sides. We used a pineapple can. Look closely at other cans before purchasing them. You can feel the ridges under the label.

1 Empty the contents and remove the label from the can. Clean, then dry the can. Fill the can with water and put it in the freezer. Wait until the water turns to ice.

2 Trace the punched-tin pattern from page 79 onto tracing paper. Cut out the pattern along the solid line.

3 Remove the can from the freezer. Wrap the pattern around the can. Fasten the pattern edges together with the transparent tape. Use the rubber bands to hold the pattern in place along the can's edges.

As the candle burns, the can may get hot. So always set your tin-can holder on a heat-safe base, such as a trivet, when the candle is burning. Be careful, too, not to touch the can while the candle is burning.

4 Make a pad with the towel. Place the can on the towel. Use the hammer and nail to punch holes through the dots and into the can. When all the holes are punched, remove the pattern. Let the water melt. Pour out the water and dry the can.

5 Spray the inside and outside of the can with the paint primer. Let the primer dry. Spray the inside and outside of the can with the white enamel paint. Let the paint dry. Wrap the ribbon around the top of the can and tie a bow. Put the candle in the can.

Snowflakes

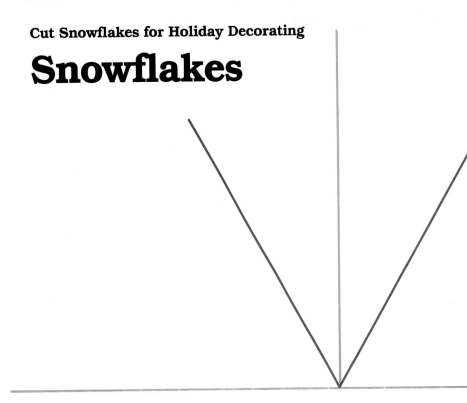

Follow these simple steps for making perfect paper snowflakes...

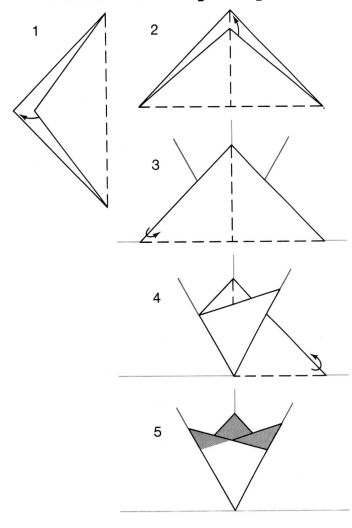

Cut your paper into any size square. We used 6-inch, 3-inch, and 2½-inch squares of typing paper for our snowflakes. Origami paper is already cut into squares when you purchase it.

1 Referring to Drawing 1, fold one paper square in half diagonally. Then unfold it.

2 Referring to Drawing 2, fold the square in half diagonally in the other direction. Do not unfold. The center of your triangle should have a crease.

3 Referring to Drawing 3, lay your triangle on the diagram above. Place the long leg of the triangle on the horizontal blue line and the crease on the vertical blue line.

4 Referring to Drawing 4, lift the left corner and crease the paper at the red line on the left.

5 Referring to Drawing 5, lift the right corner and crease the paper at the red line on the right. Cut away the shaded area of the folded square. You are now ready to cut the design of your snowflake and unfold it. Have fun.

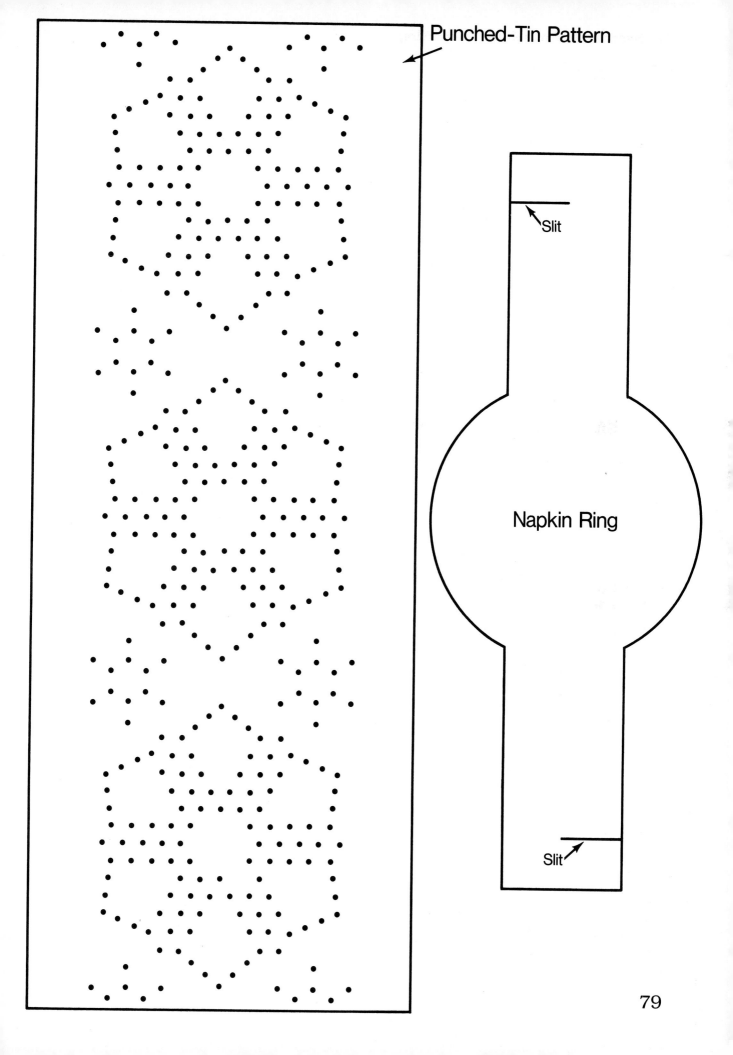

Punched-Tin Pattern

Slit

Napkin Ring

Slit

79

ACKNOWLEDGMENTS

We would like to extend our special thanks to the following designers who contributed projects to this book. When more than one project appears on a page, the acknowledgment cites both the project and the page number. A page number alone indicates one designer contributed all of the projects on that page.

Susan Carson—44–45, button wreaths and
    paper-animal ornaments
Phyllis Dunstan—4–5, 18–19
Linda Emmerson—44–45, wooden ornaments
Kathy Engel—60–61
Mary Helen Grace—52–53
Cynthia Kirk—38–39, pinwheel bows
Margaret Leonardo—72–73
Sara Jane Treinen—31, clay-pot bells;
    38–39, gift bags
Karen Ann Wiant—30–31, felt holly wreath
Dee Wittmack—10–11

We also are pleased to acknowledge the photographer whose talents and technical skills contributed much to this book.

Hopkins Associates

For their cooperation and courtesy, we extend a special thanks to the following sources.

Hallmark Cards, Inc.
Kansas City, MO 64141

Papercraft Corp.
Papercraft Park
Pittsburgh, PA 15238